The Farm

Favorite Literature and Great Activities to Spark Learning Across the Curriculum

by Lorrie L. Birchall

**THIS BELONGS TO
BARB HILL**

SCHOLASTIC
PROFESSIONAL BOOKS

New York • Toronto • London • Auckland • Sydney

For LeAnn and Alvo Moore,
the two finest teachers I know.
With much love and appreciation.
L.

Cover design by Jaime Lucero and Vincent Ceci
Cover illustration by Stephanie Peterson
Interior design by Sydney Wright
Interior illustrations by James Graham Hale

ISBN 0-590-53543-9

12 11 10 9 8 7 6 5 4 3 2 1   6 7 8 9/9/01/0

Table of Contents

Dear Teacher,

I've always found that thematic teaching provides a terrific way to incorporate listening, speaking, reading, and writing into subjects across the curriculum. What better topic to do that with than the farm! Not only can you make meaningful connections between subject areas from science to art, but concepts and skills can be introduced as extensions of literature, rather than in isolation. With this thematic unit about the farm, your students will learn and thrive!

I selected several different genres of literature for *The Farm* to enhance children's appreciation for the wonderful variety of quality children's books. The types of books include folktale, fable, fantasy and nonfiction, among others. Each literature selection acts as a catalyst for teaching specific concepts related to the theme, such as farm-animal classification and farm life in history.

As a classroom teacher, it is always my goal to develop activities that are easy for you to implement as well as stimulating and fun for your students. I hope *The Farm* helps you to plan meaningful learning experiences for the unique group of individuals in your classroom.

Lorrie L. Birchall

Increasing Comprehension Through
Reading Strategies

■ Introduction ■

You can help your students become more involved in their reading and understand books more deeply by presenting reading strategies to them before and after they read a story. I have found that the strategies in this chapter help my students become active readers—of books about the farm as well as any other topic.

In the strategies discussed below, you will find many examples that relate to words and concepts associated with the topic of this book. For each I have indicated whether they are best presented as prereading strategies, as postreading strategies, or as both.

Prereading strategies are a very important part of a literature-based reading program. Whether these strategies take the form of questioning, brainstorming, webbing, listing, or other activities, they help students develop a readiness to read. By making predictions about the text, students are able to use their own valuable life experiences to interpret and bring meaning to the text.

As a follow-up to a story, postreading strategies are important for evaluating student comprehension and extending the literature into other subject areas. When students bring meaning to the text, they can make further learning connections.

■ Strategies That Work ■

1. Questioning *(For Prereading)* Before reading a book with the class, use some of these questions to generate discussion. Children will find that they already have knowledge and some experience about the topic.

- What is the title of the book?
- Who is the author of the book?
- Who is the illustrator?
- What does the cover tell you about the book?
- How many pages are in the book?
- What is the copyright date of the book? How many years ago was it published?
- Where do you think the story takes place? What makes you say that?
- Do you think this will be a realistic story or a fantasy?
- What do you think this story is about?
- What are you curious to find out about the story?

2. Listing *(For Prereading and Postreading)* Make this simple chart on a large sheet of butcher paper. As a class, brainstorm ideas, questions, facts, and experiences and list them on the chart. Then talk about the list.

For example, before reading a nonfiction book about pigs, children may contribute these ideas:

What I know about pigs
- Pigs oink
- Pigs like mud.

What I want to know about pigs
- What do pigs on a farm like to eat?
- How many piglets does a mother usually have?

After reading a book on the subject, children may contribute to this chart:

What I learned about pigs
- Pigs like to eat corn.
- A mother pig often gives birth to between 6 and 15 piglets twice a year.

3. Webbing *(For Prereading and Postreading)* With this activity, children brainstorm words related to the central concept. As children contribute ideas about the subject or subtopics, you can record them in the appropriate spot on the

"web." To help them generate ideas, you can ask questions. For example, if the class is brainstorming everything they know about barnyard animals, you may encourage still further ideas with questions such as "What kinds of birds might we find in a barnyard?" or "What kinds of foods might be fed to barnyard animals?"

In one classroom that was about to read *Big Red Barn* by Margaret Wise Brown, the web looked like this. Your web will be based on the answers given by your students.

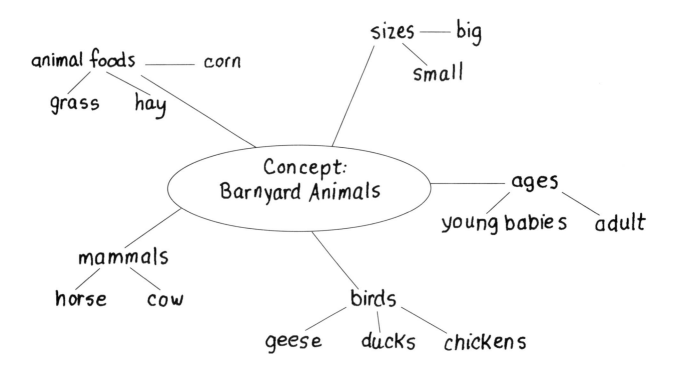

4. Examples and Nonexamples (*For Prereading or Postreading*) As a class, brainstorm some examples and nonexamples of a specific farm concept. This simple strategy will help you to determine the level of understanding your students have about a specific farm concept. Also, your students are given an opportunity to make important learning connections between new information and their own background knowledge.

In the example given here, you would ask students to mention animals on a farm and animals that would not be found on a farm.

Concept: Farm Animals

Examples	Nonexamples
cow	elephant
pig	zebra
turkey	kangaroo
horse	giraffe
sheep	koala

Other concepts to try:

farm states/nonfarm states

farm produce/nonfarm produce

farm chores/nonfarm chores

farm equipment/nonfarm equipment

farm occupations/nonfarm occupations

farm clothing/nonfarm clothing

As a cooperative learning activity, you can provide each group with a different farm concept, then ask them to generate examples and nonexamples on a chart. Each group can then share their ideas with the class. The next strategies are effective for making comparisons.

5. Compare and Contrast Through Venn Diagrams *(For Prereading or Postreading)*

1. Illustrate how Venn diagrams show comparisons between things. Provide examples.

2. Ask the students to develop the Venn diagrams individually or in cooperative learning groups.

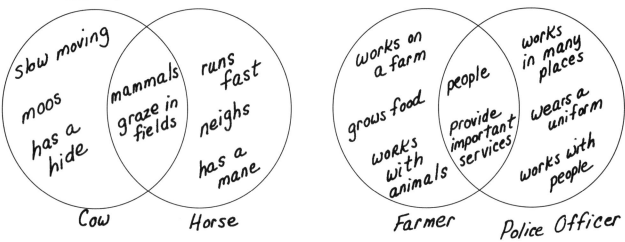

6. Making Connections *(For Postreading)*

1. List vocabulary words from the literature selection.

2. Have students think of connections between the words, focusing on relationships between them.

FORMAT:
I would connect _____ with _____ because...

Example:
Vocabulary words from "The Three Little Pigs" by James Marshall

dinner	turnips	building	wolf	straw	sticks
fair	gobbled	house	apples	boiling	bricks

I would connect <u>turnips</u> with <u>apples</u> because both are foods that are grown.
I would connect <u>turnips</u> with <u>wolf</u> because both were boiled in a pot.

7. Character Analysis *(For Postreading)*

1. Read the literature selection to the class.

2. Discuss the difference between **physical traits** and **personality traits**.

Physical traits Describe a character's outward appearance, such as brown eyes, sharp teeth, blond hair.

Personality traits Describe a character's nature, such as being sweet, kind, intelligent, clever.

3. On a chart, list the physical and personality traits for the characters in the story.

EXAMPLE for *The Town Mouse & the Country Mouse:*

CHARACTERS	PHYSICAL TRAITS	PERSONALITY TRAITS
The Town Mouse	fancy clothes	adventurous
The Country Mouse	simple clothes	enjoys simple pleasures

4. As a class, compare traits. What were some different words used to describe each character? Is it more difficult to think of words to describe physical traits or personality traits? Why?

> **Extensions:**
> - Are the describing words nouns, adjectives, or verbs?
> - Discuss the use of personification (nonhuman characters with human qualities and characteristics).
> - Write one or two complete sentences for each character using the describing words from the lists above.

8. Story Map *(For Postreading)*

1. Read the literature selection to the class.

2. On a large chart complete the story map as a class. (See page 12.) You may wish to incorporate pictures as well as words and sentences in the story map.

3. Display the story map on a classroom wall for future reference.

Example: *The Three Little Pigs*

SETTING

When?

Where?

CHARACTERS

1. _____

2. _____

3. _____

4. _____

PROBLEM

Event 1

↓

Event 2

↓

Event 3

↓

SOLUTION

Literature Units

This chart shows ten literature selections and the concepts covered in each book. These are listed according to genre (type of book).

FICTION	*Big Red Barn*	• There are many kinds of animals on the farm. • Farm animals are raised for food and other products. • Adult and baby animals have special names.
	The Day Jimmy's Boa Ate the Wash (Humor)	• Farm animals
	Rosie's Walk (Humor)	• Animals as predators and prey
	Ox-Cart Man (Historical Fiction)	• Historical look at farming • Duties on the farm • Seasons on the farm
FACT-BASED FICTION	*The Popcorn Book*	• Importance of grains • Facts about popcorn
	Eating the Alphabet	• Farms grow healthy food. • Vast array of fruits and vegetables are named.
FANTASY	*Cloudy With a Chance of Meatballs*	• Where food comes from • Importance of farmers • The role weather plays in farming
FABLE	*The Town Mouse & the Country Mouse*	• Comparison of urban and rural lifestyles • Appreciation of differences
	The Little Red Hen	• Process of growing wheat • Reaping the rewards of your labor • Helping others
FOLKTALE	*The Three Little Pigs*	• Animals as predators and prey • Animals as part of the food chain

Big Red Barn

by Margaret Wise Brown
pictures by Felicia Bond
HarperCollins, [1956] 1989

Summary: There are many animals living in the big red barn.

Language Arts:

■ Discuss the meaning of the adage: "Don't count your chickens before they're hatched!"

Synonyms: What words mean the same as *big*?

Antonyms: What words mean the opposite of *big*?

Categorization: Categorize the animals in the story by their color. Example: old black cat, big red dog, big brown cow, little black bats

Context: Using the context of the story, what words make sense in the blanks?

"Only the _____ were left to play,

Rustling and _____ in the hay,

While the moon _____ high

In the _____ night sky."

Dictionary usage: Find the word *scarecrow* in the dictionary. What is its definition?

Parts of speech: Which words name something?

| barn | bantam | eggs | little | animals |
| big | squeaking | sailed | nests | flew |

Structural analysis: Which words have the same /e/ sound as in *nests*?

| sweet | rest | green | red | eggs | hen |
| sheep | geese | ten | end | went | sleeping |

Rhyming: Think of some words that rhyme with *red*.

Critical Thinking:

1. How does this story seem realistic/unrealistic?
2. How is the big red barn similar to/different from your home?
3. Why is it important that there are so many different kinds of animals?
4. "An old scarecrow
   Was leaning on his hoe
   And a field mouse was born
   In a field of corn."
   Which farm animals are born?
   Which farm animals are hatched?

Writing:
- Write a story about which farm animal you would want to be and why.

Math:
- Count the eggs laid by the bantam hen. How many more are needed to make a dozen?
- Farms are measured in acres. What is an acre? Why do farmers plant their crops in rows? Why not triangles?

Science:
- Animals are either plant eaters (herbivores), meat eaters (carnivores), or a combination of the two (omnivores). Which farm animals, if any, are herbivores? carnivores? omnivores?

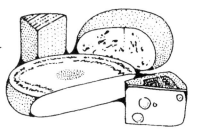

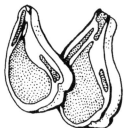

- Farm animals are raised for food and other products. List some of the products that come from farm animals.

Music/Movement:
- Make farm animal sounds and their accompanying movements.
- Learn a simple square dance and have a barn dance!

The Day Jimmy's Boa Ate the Wash

by Trinka Hakes Noble
pictures by Stephen Kellogg
Puffin, [1980] 1993

Summary: A class field trip to the farm leads to a series of silly events.

Language Arts:

Synonyms: What words mean the same as *ate?*

Antonyms: What words mean the opposite of *sad?*

Categorization: Make a web of words that have something in common with the category *wash.*

Homonyms: What are other spellings/meanings for the words *yard* and *past?*

Context: Using the context of the story, what words make sense in the blanks?

"We _____ in such a hurry that one of the _____ didn't get off the _____, so now he's got a pet."

Dictionary usage: Find the word *farm* in the dictionary. What is its definition?

Parts of speech: Which words show action?

cow	crying	haystack	yelling
eggs	eating	threw	boa

Structural analysis: Which words have the same /e/ sound as in *eggs*?

we	Jenny	she	fell
pet	hen	eating	meet

Rhyming: Think of some words that rhyme with *snake.*

Critical Thinking:

1. Why didn't the chickens like Jimmy's pet boa constrictor?

2. What was your favorite part of the story? Why?

3. Jimmy had a pet snake and then a pet pig. What are some other unusual kinds of pets?

4. Discuss the emotions felt by the farmer and the farmer's wife during the children's class trip to the farm. How were their emotions different?

5. How was this story realistic? How was it unrealistic?

6. What would you most like to see on a farm?

Writing:

■ As a class, write letters to Chambers of Commerce in farm communities requesting information about rural areas.

■ Write another ending to the story.

Math:

■ Count all the animals in the story.

■ Make a pie chart showing the number of pigs, chickens, snakes, etc.

Science:

■ Categorize the animals in the story (for example, reptiles, mammals, birds).

Art:

■ From scraps of construction paper, design a really unusual place to keep farm animals. (What if there weren't any barns?)

Social Studies:

■ If possible, take a field trip to a farm or arrange for a guest speaker who can discuss some aspect of farming. Possibilities: farmer, large-animal veterinarian, crop duster, hydroponics scientist, 4-H club member, agriculturalist, etc.

Rosie's Walk

 by Pat Hutchins
Macmillan, [1968] 1971

Summary: Rosie went for a walk, unaware of the fox trailing behind her.

Language Arts:

Synonyms: What words mean the same as *walk?*

Antonyms: What words mean the opposite of *predator?*

Categorization: Map words that have something in common with the category *prey.*

```
        meat  eat  attack
          \    |    /
trick —— prey —— predator
          /    \
        food   nature
```

Homonyms: What are other spellings/meanings for the words *yard and past?*

Context: Using the context of the story, what words make sense in the blanks?

Rosie the _____ went for a _____ across the _____ .

Dictionary usage: Find the words *hen* and *fox* in the dictionary. What are their definitions?

Parts of speech: Which words name something?

hen	yard	over	mill	fence
across	pond	past	under	haystack

Structural analysis: Which words have the same /o/ sound as in *Rosie?*

through	got	pond	over

Rhyming: Think of some words that rhyme with *hen.*

Critical Thinking:

1. Why was the fox following Rosie?
2. How was Rosie able to get back in time for dinner?
3. How would you feel if you were the fox?
4. Where could Rosie walk next time?

Writing:

■ Following the story's pattern, have students write and illustrate a story of their own.

> Example: JEREMY'S JOG
> Jeremy the kid went for a jog
> across the field
> around the pool
> over the bridge
> past the school
> through the tunnel
> under the fence
> and got back in time for soccer practice.

Math:

■ Make paper-plate clocks and show how much time you think Rosie was gone on her walk. What time of day did Rosie go on her walk?

Science:

■ Discuss the predator/prey relationship between Rosie the hen and the fox.

Movement:

Devise a simple obstacle course in your classroom to move through the same actions of the story.

> Example: walk *around* the chair
> step *over* the blocks
> walk *through* the door

Ox-Cart Man

 by Donald Hall
pictures by Barbara Cooney
Puffin, 1983

Summary: The story describes farm life for an early nineteenth century New England family throughout the year.

Language Arts:

- Analyze the setting and time period of the story.
- What are some of the picture clues that show when and where the story takes place? (examples: clothing styles, types of transportation)

Synonyms: What words mean the same as *walked?*

Antonyms: What words mean the opposite of *soft?*

Categorization: Map words that have something in common with the category *market.*

Homonyms: What are other spellings/meanings for the words *pair* and *nose?*

Context: Using the context of the story, what words make sense in the blanks?

"He packed a bag of _____ he sheared form the _____ in April."

Dictionary usage: Find the word *market* in the dictionary. What is its definition?

Parts of speech: Which words show action?

feathers	embroidered	sheared	peppermint	sheep
knitted	candles	carved	cabbages	valleys

Structural analysis: Which words have the same /e/ sound as in *sheep?*

wheel	linen	seed	kettle	he
trees	ten	new	needle	geese

Critical Thinking:

1. Compared with today, how was life more difficult/easier for farm families living in the nineteenth century?

2. How is your life different from/similar to that of the ox-cart man's family?

3. Does the farm family in the story seem happy? Why/Why not?

4. What are some other good titles for this story?

Writing:

■ As a class, write a list of the many action words (verbs) mentioned in the story. (examples: packed, sheared, wove, spun, carved, tapped, boiled)

Math:

■ Using the clues from the story, estimate how many days the ox-cart man was gone from his family.

■ The ox-cart man bought two pounds of wintergreen peppermint candies for his family. How many pieces is that? To make it last a year, how often would each family member get a piece?

■ Ration out two pounds of wintergreen peppermint candies for the class.

■ Make a timeline from the early nineteenth century to today. Approximately how many years have passed since that time?

Science/Social Studies:

■ Each family member was responsible for making important contributions through all four seasons. On a chart, list the family's duties performed throughout the year.

■ Draw a map of the ox-cart man's journey walking "over hills, through valleys, by streams, past farms and villages until he came to Portsmouth and Portsmouth Market."

■ Locate Portsmouth, New Hampshire on a United States map.

The Popcorn Book

by Tomie de Paola
Holiday House, 1978

Summary: Factual information about popcorn is presented humorously.

Language Arts:

■ Popcorn is a compound word. List some other compound words within the category of food (for example, milkshakes, blueberries, meatballs, popsicles).

Synonyms: What words mean the same as *grow*?

Antonyms: What words mean the opposite of *grow*?

Categorization: Map words that have something in common with the category *popcorn*.

Homonyms: What are other spellings/meanings for *kernel*?

Dictionary usage: Find the word *popcorn* in the dictionary. What is its definition?

Parts of speech: Which words name something?

| Columbus | hot | popped | jewelry | stir |
| Indians | eating | breakfast | colonists | sweet |

Context: Using the context of the story, what words make sense in the blanks?

"One of the first sights _____ saw in the New _____ was the Indians in San Salvador selling _____ and wearing it as _____."

Structural Analysis: Which words have the same /o/ sound as in *pop*?

| go | lot | fond | old | top |

Rhyming: Think of some words that rhyme with *pop*.

Critical Thinking:

1. What are the three main types of corn? Which kind do people eat?
2. Who discovered popcorn?
3. What were some different ways of popping popcorn?
4. Why does popcorn pop?

Writing:

- The Indian people had a legend that a little demon lived inside popcorn kernels. Write unique and fun legends about popcorn.
- List as many kinds of foods as possible that are made with corn.

Math:

- According to the book, "Today, Americans use 500,000,000 pounds of popcorn each year. Thirty percent is eaten at movies, circuses, ball games, and county fairs. Ten percent is saved for seed and sold to other countries. But sixty percent is popped at home." Make a large pie chart illustrating these percentages.
- Estimate the number of corn kernels in a glass jar.
- Compare the weight and volume of popcorn kernels before and after popping.

Social Studies:

- Locate the top popcorn-eating cities of Milwaukee and Minneapolis on a U.S. map. These are followed by Chicago and Seattle. Which of these cities is not in the midwest?
- Find out where the "corn belt" is located on a United States map. What conditions make that area so important for growing corn?

Art:

- String popcorn into jewelry like the Indians in San Salvador did.

Music/Movement:

- Make musical shakers from popcorn kernels and recycled containers, such as lunch milk cartons and empty oatmeal boxes.
- Act out a popcorn kernel in a hot pan becoming popcorn.

Eating the Alphabet

Fruits and Vegetables From A to Z

by Lois Ehlert
Harcourt Brace, 1989

Summary: Colorful fruits and vegetables are introduced from A to Z.

Language Arts:

Synonyms: What words mean the same as *eating?*

Antonyms: What words mean the opposite of *sweet?*

Categorization:
- Categorize the foods in the story as fruits or vegetables.
- Categorize the fruits and vegetables by color.

Homonyms: What are other spellings/meanings for *pear?*

Dictionary usage: Find the word *fruit* and *vegetable* in the dictionary. What are their definitions?

Parts of speech: Which words name something?

blueberry	eating	lemon	watermelon

Structural analysis: Which words have the same /i/ sound as in *fig?*

artichoke	cauliflower	zucchini
broccoli	jicama	radish

Rhyming: Think of some words that rhyme with *beet.*

Critical Thinking:

1. What are some fruits and vegetables from the book that you are familiar with? What are some that you have not yet tried?
2. What does it mean if a person is a *vegetarian?*
3. What is your favorite fruit? Vegetable?

Math:

- Have students observe the various shapes and colors of seeds from fruit and vegetable seed packets. (Packets of seeds are inexpensive and readily available at home and garden centers.)
- Compare the sizes of seeds. Then sequence the seeds from smallest to largest. Glue the sequence of seeds on a chart labeled with the seed names.
- Count the number of fruits and vegetables in the book.

Science:

- Why is it important for people to eat a variety of fruits and vegetables?
- Grow various fruits and vegetables from seeds. Chart their growth.
- Learn about new technologies in growing food. Example: There is no soil involved with hydroponic farming. Nutrients are given to the plant through water.

Social Studies:

- Learn more about the geographic origins for each of the fruits and vegetables by reading the glossary in the back of the book. Why aren't all fruits and vegetables grown in the same place?
- On a world map locate where the various fruits and vegetables are grown.

Art:

- Using various seeds and their seed packets, create a class collage on a large sheet of oaktag or on a bulletin board.

Cooking:

- Your students will enjoy these edible ABC's. To make them, you'll need: Four 3-oz. packages of any fruit–flavored gelatin; 2 1/2 cups boiling water; alphabet-shaped cookie cutters. What to do: Stir boiling water into gelatin. Make sure it dissolves completely. Pour mixture into a 9- by 13-inch pan. Refrigerate 3 to 4 hours. Dip the bottom of the pan in warm (not hot) water for 15 seconds to loosen the gelatin. Cut out the letters with alphabet cookie cutters.

Cloudy With a Chance of Meatballs

by Judi Barrett
pictures by Ron Barrett
Macmillan, [1978] 1982

Summary: In the tiny town of Chewandswallow, food falls from the sky at predictable meal times—until the "weather" takes a turn for the worse!

Language Arts:

- Discuss the meaning of the idiom "It's raining cats and dogs."
- Read weather predictions from the newspaper.

Synonyms: What words mean the same thing as *cloudy*?

Antonyms: What words mean the opposite of *clean*?

Categorization: Map words that have something in common with the category *rain*.

Homonyms: What are other spellings/meanings for the words *weather* and *rain*?

Context: Using the context of the story, what words make sense in the blanks?

"It snowed _____ and _____. And sometimes the wind blew in storms of _____."

Dictionary usage: Find the word *prediction* in the dictionary. What is its definition?

Parts of speech: Which words name something?

clouds	meatballs	drizzled	Jell-O
storm	raining	cloudy	cheese

Structural analysis: Which words have the same /a/ sound as in *mashed?*

> hamburger rained frankfurters
> baked   and   chance

Critical Thinking:

1. Would you like to live in the town of Chewandswallow? Explain.

2. Why weren't there any farmers in the town of Chewandswallow? Why are farmers so important in real life?

3. After the Sanitation Department fed the animals, they put the rest of the food into the earth to make the soil "richer." How do farmers make the soil richer for growing food? (Discuss the use of fertilizers.)

4. What foods would you want to fall from the sky?

5. Why is this story considered a fantasy?

Writing:

■ Have students write their own weather predictions.

Math:

■ Measure 15 inches to show the height of the drifts of cream cheese and jelly sandwiches.

■ Graph the temperature highs and lows in your community for at least a week.

Science:

■ The headline in the Chewandswallow Digest said, "Spaghetti Ties Up Town!" Discuss how extreme weather conditions affect the crops that farmers grow (tornadoes, droughts, floods).

Social Studies:

■ What are the weather conditions necessary to grow potatoes in Idaho? Pineapples in Hawaii? Corn in Nebraska?

Art:

■ From recycled materials, invent machines to collect different foods falling from the sky. Have students name the machines and describe how they work.

The Town Mouse & the Country Mouse

by Lorinda Bryan Cauley
Putnam, [1984] 1990

Summary: The Town Mouse visits his cousin in the country. Then the Country Mouse visits the Town Mouse. Each has a unique perspective of the other's lifestyle.

Language Arts:

Synonyms: What words mean the same as *supper?*

Antonyms: What words mean the opposite of *hungry?*

Categorization: Map words that have something in common with the category *setting.*

Homonyms: What are other spellings/meanings for the words *through* and *hole?*

Context: Using the context of the story, what words make sense in the blanks?

"They went through the _____ room and into the dining room and there on a _____ table was the remains of a fine _____."

Dictionary usage: Find the word *perspective* in the dictionary. What is its definition?

Parts of speech: Which words show action?

town	cracked	soup	scampering
country	barking	dogs	gathered

Rhyming: Think of some words that rhyme with *town.*

Structural Analysis: Which words have the same /u/ sound as in *cup*?

> supper   snug   soup   hungry   you   nutcake

Critical Thinking:

1. Look at the picture clues. When did the story take place?

2. How is life in the country the same today? How is it different?

3. How is life in town (cities) the same today? How is it different?

4. How did each mouse react to living a different lifestyle?

5. Have you ever been to a place that is very different from where you live? How did you react?

4. What things would you absolutely need to live in the country? What could you live without? What things would you absolutely need to live in the city? What could you live without?

Writing:

■ Write the letter from the Country Mouse that convinced his cousin the Town Mouse to visit. Have students use letter writing format.

Math/Social Studies:

■ Discuss the map symbols relating to the population size of an area. These are good clues to whether an area is urban or rural. What does *suburban* mean?

■ Using a map, calculate the distance in miles (or kilometers) between an urban and rural area in your state.

Art:

■ Divide a bulletin board in half. Using recycled materials and scraps of colored construction paper, invite students to create a city collage on one side and a country collage on the other.

Music:

■ Music genres are greatly influenced by urban and rural areas. Listen to some appropriate "Country Music" and "Rap Music." How are these styles of music similar/different?

The Little Red Hen

by Paul Galdone
Clarion, [1973] 1985

Summary: The Little Red Hen does not get any help tending the wheat, so she ends up doing all the work herself—and reaps the reward.

Language Arts:

Synonyms: What words mean the same as *sleep?*

Antonyms: What words mean the opposite of *lazy?*

Categorization: Map words that have something in common with the category *wheat.*

Homonyms: What are other spellings/meanings for the word *flour?*

Context: Using the context of the story, what words make sense in the blanks?

> "She gathered _____ and made a fire in the _____. Then she took milk and sugar and eggs and butter and _____ them in a big _____ with the fine white flour."

Dictionary usage: Find the word *help* in the dictionary. What is its definition?

Parts of speech: Which words show action?

planted	tended	chair	gathered	built
sunny	mixed	hen	scampered	cake
mouse	warm	wheat	watered	she

Structural Analysis: Which words have the same /e/ sound as in *red?*

hen	sleep	she	weeds	swept	wheat	eggs
smell	eat	tended	leaves	three	helpers	cake

Rhyming: Think of some words that rhyme with *hen.*

Critical Thinking:

1. Have students think of three food items made from wheat.

2. Ask students to bring in a variety of cereal boxes to compare nutrition panels.

3. Why is it important to help others? How do you help others? Do you ever offer to help without being asked first?

4. How could the Little Red Hen have asked her friends in such a manner that they would have helped her? (e.g., Would you rather plant the wheat or cut the wheat?)

5. Do you think the Little Red Hen should have shared her cake? Why? Why not?

6. Have you ever known anyone like the cat, the dog and the mouse? Explain.

Social Studies:

■ Locate on a United States map some areas where wheat is grown.

Writing:

■ Most nutritious cereals are made primarily from grains. Brainstorm the names of cereals with the grain mentioned in the name (e.g., Wheaties, Corn Flakes, Rice Krispies).

■ Write up a "Chore Chart" for the cat, dog, mouse, and the Little Red Hen to divide up the housework evenly.

The Three Little Pigs

by James Marshall
Dial, 1989

Summary: Three little pigs each build a house from a different building material. But only one pig avoids becoming the wolf's dinner.

Language Arts:

Synonyms: What words mean the same as *hungry?*

Antonyms: What words mean the opposite of *mean?*

Categorization: Map words that have something in common with the category *house.*

Homonyms: What are other spellings/meanings for the words *fair* and *blue?*

Context: Using the context of the story, what words make sense in the blanks?

"The first little _____ met a man with a load of _____.

Dictionary usage: Find the words *predator* and *prey* in the dictionary. What are their definitions?

Parts of speech: Which words show action?

| loitering | huffed | gobbled | turnips |
| cooked | pot | pig | wolf |

Structural Analysis: Which words have the same /i/ sound as in *pig?*

Rhyming: Think of some words that rhyme with *house.*

Critical Thinking:

1. Why couldn't the three pigs and the wolf be friends?

2. When the third little pig built his house, "it took him quite a bit of time, but it was well worth it." Why was it well worth it? When have you spent a lot of time doing something that was well worth it?

3. How was the wolf smart and cunning? How was the third pig smart and cunning?

4. The wolf "gobbled up" the first two pigs and the third pig "gobbled up" the wolf. What are some other action words to describe how the pig could have eaten the wolf (e.g., consumed, devoured, chewed, etc.)

5. What are some unusual foods you have eaten?

Math:

- Estimate the amount of time it took each pig to build his house.
- As a class, write simple subtraction problems based on the story.
  Examples: 3 pigs - 1 pig = 2 pigs left
  2 pigs - 1 pig = 1 pig left
  1 wolf - 1 wolf = 0 wolves left

Science:

- Discuss how predators and prey are part of the food chain. (A predator is an animal that survives by hunting others. Prey is any creature that is hunted or caught for food.) The wolf is a predator and the pigs were his prey. How did the wolf end up becoming prey?
- Are farm animals predators or prey? Can an animal be both a predator and prey? How, if at all, are humans predators/prey?

Social Studies:

- Learn about different kinds of houses built around the world (for example, castles in Bavaria, igloos in Alaska, earth-covered homes in Norway).
- List all the different materials that can be used to build a house.

Art:

- From recycled materials, such as milk cartons and oatmeal containers, build a sturdy house for one of the three pigs. Decorate it with construction paper scraps, paint, markers. Blow on the house. Does it stand up? If not what can you use to make it more sturdy?

Language Arts

■ Vocabulary ■

farm	grain	seed	egg	vegetable	cow
grow	harvest	pig	silo	cat	hay
fruit	horse	dog	wheat	meat	chicken
barn	corn	sun	duck	acre	land

Alphabetize Farm Words Select as many appropriate words from the above list as your students can handle. Write each farm vocabulary word on a 3-by 5-inch index card. Have students work in pairs or groups to put some of the words in ABC order. Example:

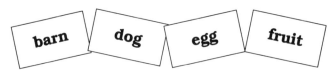

Something in Common Give cooperative learning groups a few of the farm vocabulary words written on the index cards. Have students pair up the words—but each pair must have something in common. Share the ideas.

Possibilities:	cat	and	corn	Both start with the letter *c*.
	fruit	and	vegetable	Both are healthy foods.
	horse	and	grain	Both are 5-letter words.

Grow Farm Sentences In cooperative groups, challenge students to verbalize sentences to include two, three, or more farm vocabulary words.
Examples: The *chicken* likes to eat *corn*.
　　　　　Wheat is a *grain* that *grows* on the *farm*.

■ Poetry Activities ■

Making Poetry Sequence Strips Write a simple farm poem or farm-theme nursery rhyme on oaktag. (See pages 36–37 for examples.) Cut the lines into strips and have students put them in correct sequence. Store the strips in a ziplock bag labeled with the poem's title.

> Example:
> Higgledy, Piggledy, my black hen
> She lays eggs for gentlemen;
> Gentlemen come every day
> To see what my black hen doth lay.

Using the Cloze Procedure On a large chart, write out a farm poem, leaving a few blank spaces. Ask students to think of words that would make sense in the blanks. Then invite volunteers to illustrate the poem and display.

> Example:
> BILLY GOAT
> There was a young goat named _____
> Who was more than a little bit _____.
> They sent him to _____.
> But he just played the _____
> And ate _____ and _____ willy-nilly.

Farm Rhymes On a large chart, have the class brainstorm rhyming words for these farm words. Then together write a simple rhyming farm poem.

cat	hen	day	cow

▦ Farm Poems ▦

by anonymous authors

A Farmer's Boy

They strolled down the land together,
The sky studded with stars—
They reached the gate in silence
And he lifted down the bars—
She neither smiled nor thanked him
Because she knew not how;
For he was just a farmer's boy
And she was a jersey cow.

I Had A Little Pig

I had a little pig,
I fed him in a trough,
He got so fat
His tail dropped off.
So I got me a hammer,
And I got me a nail,
And I made my little pig
A brand-new tail.

I'm Glad the Sky is Painted Blue

I'm glad the sky is painted blue,
And the earth is painted green,
With such a lot of nice fresh air,
All sandwiched in between.

Billy Goat

There was a young goat named Billy
Who was more than a little bit silly.
They sent him to school
But he just played the fool
And ate satchels and books willy-nilly.

Cackle, Cackle, Mother Goose

Cackle, cackle, Mother Goose,
Have you any feathers loose?
Truly have I, pretty fellow,
Half enough to fill a pillow.
Here are quills, take one or two,
And down to make a bed for you.

■ Nursery Rhymes ■

Higglety, Pigglety, Pop!

Higglety, pigglety, pop!
The dog has eaten the mop;
  The pig's in a hurry,
  The cat's in a flurry,
Higglety, pigglety, pop!

The Flying Pig

Dickery, dickery, dare,
The pig flew up in the air;
The man in brown
Soon brought him down,
Dickery, dickery, dare.

Little Bo Peep

Little Bo-peep has lost her sheep,
  And can't tell where to find them;
Leave them alone, and they'll come home,
  Bringing their tails behind them.

Bow-Wow

Bow-wow says the dog,
Mew, mew says the cat,
Grunt, grunt goes the hog,
And squeak goes the rat.

Whoo-oo says the owl,
Caw, caw says the crow,
Quack, quack says the duck,
And what cuckoos say, you know.

Baa, Baa, Black Sheep

Baa, baa, black sheep,
  Have you any wool?
Yes, sir, yes, sir,
  three bags full;
One for the master,
  And one for the dame,
And one for the little boy
  Who lives down the lane.

■ Big Book of Farm Alliteration ■

These "tongue twisters" will get your kids giggling!

Materials:

large sheets of oaktag
crayons or markers
black marker
stapler or other binding materials

Directions:

1. As a class, or in cooperative groups, write alliterations—phrases containing words that have the same initial sounds—for farm vocabulary words.

2. Illustrate each alliteration on a large sheet of oaktag.

3. Combine alliterations into a class Big Book.

Here are some possible farm vocabulary words to spark alliterations. Challenge students to come up with other possibilities, too.

A	apples, acres, agriculture	**N**	Nebraska
B	barn, bird	**O**	oink, oats
C	cow, cereal, carrots	**P**	pig, plant, plow
D	duck	**Q**	quilt, quiet
E	eggs	**R**	rain, rooster, rice
F	fruit, farm, food	**S**	scarecrow, silo, seed, sheep
G	grain, grow	**T**	tractor, turnips
H	hay, horses	**U**	udder
I	Idaho	**V**	vegetable, veterinarian
J	juice	**W**	wool, wheat, weather, wind
K	Kansas	**X**	X-L overalls
L	land	**Y**	yard
M	milk, moo	**Z**	zero, zest

▨ Similes ▨

A barnyard will come alive in your classroom when
students act out these farm similies!

Directions:

1. Explain to students that we often use animal characteristics to describe and compare ourselves. These figures of speech are called *similes*.

2. Have students illustrate each animal simile below individually or in groups.

3. Play farm animal charades: Have students act out each animal simile.

eat like a pig   legs like a chicken
cocky as a rooster   swim like a fish
strong as a bull   sing like a bird
hungry as a horse   proud as a peacock

4. As a class, think of some other animal similes.

lazy as a _____   hair like a _____
happy as a _____   nose like a _____
slow as a _____   ears like a _____
fast as a _____   teeth like a _____

▨ Analogies ▨

Sharpen your students' critical thinking skills with these farm analogies.

Directions:

1. Ask students to describe how the italicized words are related.

2. Compare the second line in the same way to complete the analogy.

3. Challenge students to come up with their own farm analogies.

1. *Oink* is to *pig*
as *moo* is to _____.
2. *Hides* are to *cows*
as _____ are to *chickens*.
3. *Chickens* are to *eggs*
as _____ are to *milk*.
4. *Farmhouse* is to *country*
as *skyscraper* is to _____.

5. *Kid* is to *goat*
as *calf* is to _____.
6. *Horse* is to *gallop*
as *bird* is to _____.
7. *Pediatrician* is to *children*
as _____ is to *animals*.
8. *Slop* is to *pigs*
as *hay* is to _____.

■ Compound Words ■

Students will get a kick out of making up crazy compound words!

Directions:

1. Cut apart these farm compound words.

2. Ask children to mix up the words to create new compound words.

sunhouse

3. Have them glue each new compound to a sheet of paper and illustrate their work.
Example: sunshine + farmhouse = sunhouse

barn	**yard**
hay	**stack**
sun	**shine**
farm	**house**
horse	**shoe**
moon	**light**
scare	**crow**

■ Growing Verbs ■

"Grow" verbs in your class by adding the suffix -ing to farm root words!

Materials:

green construction paper
yellow construction paper
black marker
stapler or other binding materials
8 1/2- by 11-inch sheet of
    oaktag for each book page
scissors

FARM ROOT WORDS WITH THE SUFFIX -ING
planting   milking   growing   raining
feeding   plowing   husking   eating

Directions:

1. Have each cooperative group make a pull-tab cornstalk using one farm root word with the suffix -ing.

2. Brainstorm sentences using the farm verbs.

3. Have each cooperative group write one sentence using their farm verb on a sheet of oaktag.

4. Compile the pages into a class book.

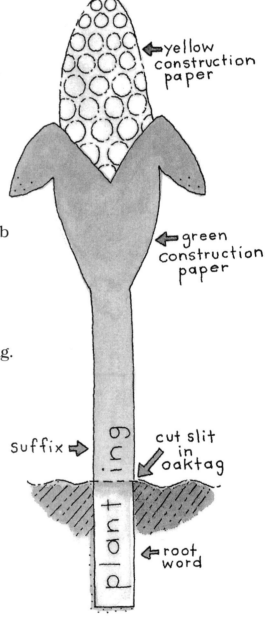

yellow construction paper

green construction paper

suffix ➡

cut slit in oaktag

root word

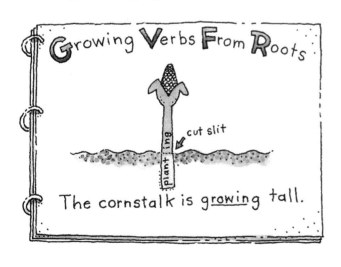

Growing Verbs From Roots

cut slit

The cornstalk is growing tall.

■ Farmer's Vowel Pockets ■

This activity gives students practice in distinguishing
between long and short vowel sounds.

Directions:

1. As a class, review long and short vowel sounds.

2. Make five copies of the Farmer's Pockets page.

3. Cut two construction-paper or oaktag pockets to fit the pocket shapes on each page. Glue these to each page.

4. Write one set of long and short vowels on each Farmer's Pockets page. Example:

5. For added appeal, color the page. Then glue each page to a piece of oaktag (for example, half of a file folder).

6. Laminate each Farmer's Pocket page for durability. Then cut a slit across each pocket.

7. Copy each vocabulary word listed below on a 3- by 5-inch index card. On the back, mark the correct vowel and symbol (e.g., ā) for self-checking.

9. Farmer's Pockets and vocabulary words can be stored in a large manila envelope.

Selected Vocabulary Words:

chick	hay	grass	geese	duck	sheep
wet	hen	sun	calf	seed	egg
pig	day	cold	vet	night	hot
bull	grow	plant	milk	cheese	dig

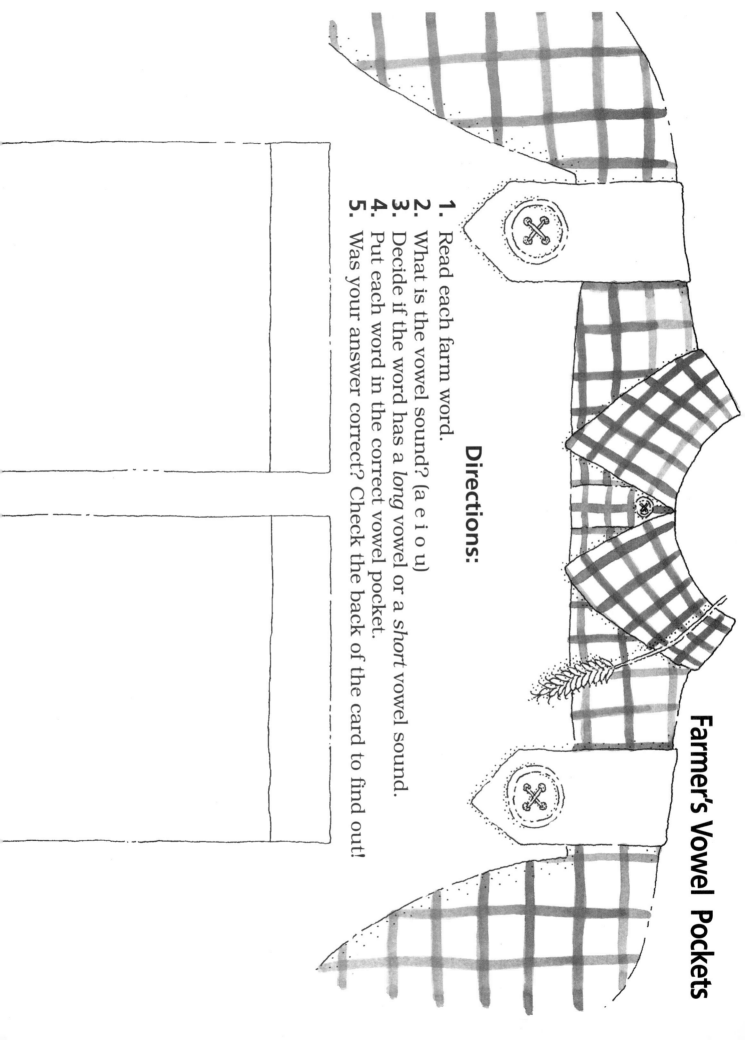

Directions:

1. Read each farm word.
2. What is the vowel sound? (a e i o u)
3. Decide if the word has a *long* vowel or a *short* vowel sound.
4. Put each word in the correct vowel pocket.
5. Was your answer correct? Check the back of the card to find out!

Farmer's Vowel Pockets

■ Rhyming Farm Animal Strips ■

Here's a fun and easy way to help your students build their vocabulary.

Directions:

1. Make one copy of this page and pages 45 and 46 for each student. Have students cut out the farm animals and their letter strips.

2. They then cut along the two dotted lines in the middle of each farm animal.

3. Students slide each letter strip through the back of the farm animal that goes with it.

4. Sudents then read all the new rhyming words.

5. Challenge them to write poems using some of these words.

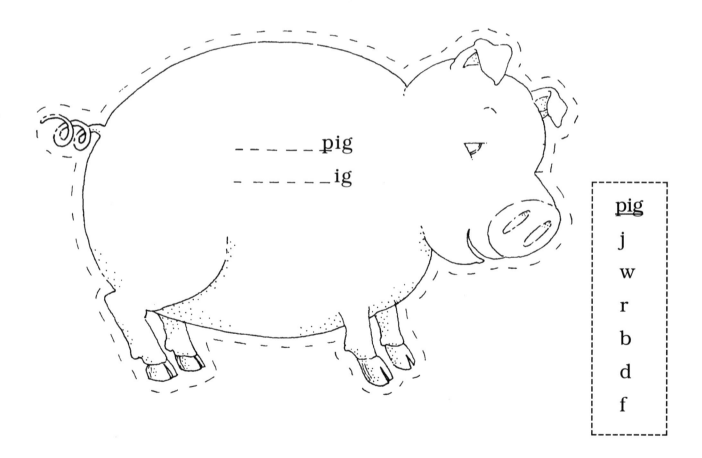

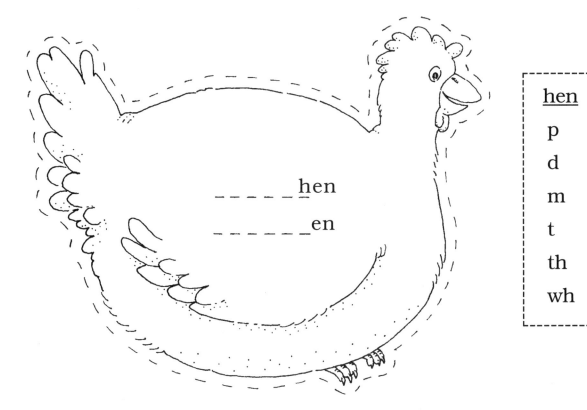

_ _ _ _ _ hen

_ _ _ _ _ en

hen
p
d
m
t
th
wh

_ _ _ _ _ cow

_ _ _ _ _ ow

cow
n
h
s
v
w
pl
b

_ _ _ _ _ <u>s</u> <u>h</u> eep

_ _ _ _ _ eep

sheep

k
b
d
j
p
w
st
cr

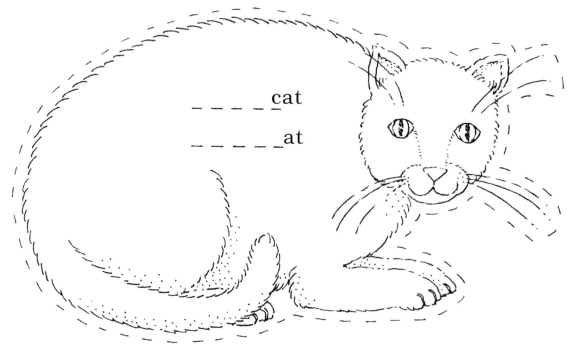

_ _ _ _ _ cat

_ _ _ _ _ at

cat

b
f
h
m
p
s
r
v

■ Farm Jokes and Activities ■

Jokes in a Reading Skills Lesson Many jokes contain excellent examples of homonyms and plays on words.

> Example: Why shouldn't you bring a pet chicken to school?
> (It might use *fowl* language.)

Jokes in a Listening Center Record the Corny Farm Jokes on an audio cassette and place in a Listening Center.

Jokes for Paired Reading In addition to being funny, jokes are meant to be shared. This provides encouragement for many reluctant and emergent readers.

Jokes as Drama Invite students to memorize a few of their favorite Corny Farm Jokes and have a stand-up comedy hour!

■ Corny Farm Jokes ■

What did the tomato tell the celery?
(Quit stalking me.)

What do you call potatoes that insult a farmer?
(fresh vegetables)

What happened when the duck heard a silly joke?
(He really quacked up.)

Why was the cornstalk angry with the farmer?
(Because the farmer kept pulling its ears.)

Who won the race between the carrot and the lettuce?
(The lettuce, because it was a-head.)

What game does the mother hen play with her chick?
(peck-a-boo)

What do cows enjoy doing on Saturday nights?
(going to the moo-vies)

What keys on a farm won't operate a tractor or open the barn door?
(donkeys and turkeys)

What do you call pigs who write letters to each other?
(pig pen pals)

Where do pigs park?
(at porking meters)

Writing

■ Barn-Shaped Writing Booklets ■

Directions:

1. Cut out the barn shape from red construction paper.

2. Staple lined writing paper to the red barn and cut around its shape.

3. The red-barn writing booklets are ready for a writing center, and individual and group writing projects.

Farm Story Starters

1. The mother hen scolded her chicks sternly for . . .

2. A new baby animal was born in the big red barn! She was a beautiful . . .

3. The animals were making such a commotion because the farmer . . .

4. The giant harvest moon was just beginning to rise over the big red barn when suddenly I heard . . .

5. I thought I saw the scarecrow make a face at me when I was . . .

6. The cows were angry with the chickens because . . .

7. Once the rooster crowed, all the animals . . .

8. Old MacDonald took the animals to the County Fair where they . . .

Animal Talk

■ ■ ■ ■ ■ ■ ■ ■ ■ ■ ■

Directions: If these farm animals could speak to you, what would they say? Write what you think in each of the speech balloons.

▪ Farmer's Diary ▪

Directions:

1. Discuss the fact that farmers have many jobs on a farm. Brainstorm all the things that a farmer must do from sunup past sundown.

2. Ask students to imagine that they are farmers. On a large chart, write a group diary entry for one day in the life of a farmer.

3. Display the diary entry on a classroom wall. Consider using the diary entry as a choral reading activity.

Date: _____ , _____

Dear Diary,

First thing this morning I _____

_____

_____

_____

_____

_____

_____

_____

Name _____

Be a Farm Reporter!

■ ■ ■ ■ ■ ■ ■ ■ ■ ■ ■ ■ ■ ■ ■ ■ ■ ■ ■

Directions:

1. Pretend that you are a newspaper reporter for *Farm World News*. Write a news story about one of the amazing fruits or vegetables listed on your *Fruit and Vegetable World Records* chart. Write your story on the lines below. (Use the back of this page if you need more space.)

2. Draw a picture to go with your story.

3. Write a catchy headline above the picture. Example: MONSTER PUMPKIN INVADES NEW JERSEY!

FARM WORLD NEWS

Vol. CXXVII NO. 32   25¢

Fruit and Vegetable World Records

■ ■

These amazing fruits and vegetables are listed in the *Guinness Book of Records*. Pick one and write a news story about it.

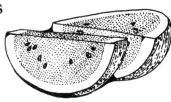

Apple	3 lb. 2 oz.	(Caro, Michigan, 1992)
Cabbage	124 lb.	(Llanharry, Great Britain, 1989)
Cantaloupe	62 lb.	(Rocky Mount, North Carolina, 1991)
Carrot	15 lb. 7 oz.	(Nelson, New Zealand, 1978)
Celery	46 lb. 1 oz.	(Llanharry, Great Britain, 1990)
Cucumber	20 lb. 1 oz.	(Llanharry, Great Britain, 1991)
Grapefruit	6 lb. 8 1/2 oz.	(Tucson, Arizona, 1984)
Onion	11 lb. 2 oz.	(Cummock, Great Britain, 1992)
Pineapple	17 lb. 8 oz.	(South Cotobato, Philippines, 1984)
Pumpkin	836 lb.	(Stouffville, Ontario, Canada, 1993)
Radish	37 lb. 15 oz.	(Tanunda, South Australia, 1992)
Rhubarb	5 lb. 14 oz.	(East Woodyates, Great Britain, 1985)
Strawberry	8.17 oz.	(Folkstone, Great Britain, 1983)
Tomato	7 lb. 12 oz.	(Edmond, Oklahoma, 1986)
Watermelon	262 lb.	(Arrington, Tennessee, 1990)

SOURCE: The Guinness Book of Records—1995 Edition
Guinness Publishing Ltd. copyright © 1994

▪ Parts of a Story Wheel ▪

Directions:

1. Cut out four large wheels from oaktag for each part of a story: SETTING, CHARACTERS, EVENTS and TIME.

2. As a class, brainstorm appropriate responses for each wheel, based upon literature selections the class has read.

3. Attach the wheels to a bulletin board with a tack for rotating.

Setting
Chewandswallow
town
country
New England
farm

Characters
children
Town mouse
Country mouse
3 Pigs
farmer
Little Red Hen
boa constrictor
Big Bad Wolf

Events
Sell food at market
children throw eggs
food into blows town
huff and puff and blow house down

Time
Autumn
morning
Colonial Days
present day

Extensions:

1. Zany Stories: Have students choose one or more selections from each wheel to write a zany story individually, in pairs, or in cooperative groups.

2. Writing Development: Once students have used familiar literature as a jumping board for understanding parts of a story, extend the activity. Have them work in cooperative groups to develop "wheels" for many possible settings, characters, events, and times to help them develop their writing. Then display the finished work.

Math

■ Math Rhymes ■

Choral Reading As a class, chant the math rhyme. Use fingers to illustrate the subtraction.

Sequencing Make ten simple felt chickens for a felt story board. Read the math rhyme and remove one chicken at a time.

Movement Invite students to perform a "rap" version of the math rhyme with accompanying movements.

Music Have students think of a melody to accompany the math rhyme. Clap the beats of the math rhyme.

Drama Ask for ten volunteers to act out the events of the math rhyme.

■ Ten Little Chickens ■
(Math Rhyme)

Ten little chickens pecking in a line
One scampered off and then there were nine.

Nine little chickens ran through the gate
One stubbed her claw and then there were eight.

Eight little chickens the oldest named Kevin
He moved to Kansas and then there were seven.

Seven little chickens jumped over sticks
One flew the coop and then there were six.

Six little chickens found a bee's hive
One got stung and then there were five.

Five little chickens scratched at the door
One hid behind it and then there were four.

Four little chickens played in a tree
One broke a branch and then there were three.

Three little chickens had nothing left to do
One ran home and then there were two.

Two little chickens weren't having fun
One waved good-bye and then there was one.

One little chicken thought she was a hero
She pranced on home and then there were zero!

▦ Sally's Patients ▦
(Making Deductions)

Directions:

1. Copy the chart below on a large sheet of butcher paper.

2. Read aloud the introduction about Dr. Sally Jones (below). Then ask students to read aloud the clues.

3. Write the name of the animal scheduled to see Dr. Jones each day on the chart.

Dr. Sally Jones is a veterinarian. Her patients are different animals on the farm. She works every day except Sunday. Listen to the clues to help figure out when the animals have their doctor appointments. (Answer: Sunday= (blank); Monday= Peggy Pig; Tuesday= Harvey Horse; Wednesday=Cleo Cow; Thursday=Terry Turkey; Friday=Clifford Cat; Saturday=Roger Rooster)

Clues:

1. Cleo Cow's appointment is Wednesday.

2. Peggy Pig's appointment is two days before Cleo's.

3. Terry Turkey's appointment is one day after Cleo's.

4. Roger Rooster's appointment is two days after Terry's.

5. Clifford Cat's appointment is one day before Roger's.

6. Harvey Horse's appointment is four days before Roger's.

Appointment Book for Dr. Sally Jones	
SUNDAY	
MONDAY	
TUESDAY	
WEDNESDAY	
THURSDAY	
FRIDAY	
SATURDAY	

■ Making Vegetable Soup ■

Ask students to each bring in one or two vegetables to do math and make soup!

Activity 1: Graphing Vegetables

1. Place a large sheet of white butcher paper on the floor.

2. Organize the vegetables into rows on the paper, creating a pictograph.

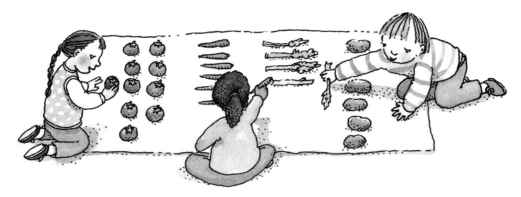

3. Ask questions about the pictograph. Examples: How many (tomatoes) are there? How many more tomatoes are there than carrots?

Activity 2: Vegetable Fractions

1. Gather ingredients to make a simple vegetable soup.

2. While preparing the vegetables for soup, cut them into designated fractions. Example: Cut the potatoes in half, then fourths, eighths, etc. Cut one carrot into five sections and another carrot into ten sections. Ask questions about the sections (fractions). Would you get a bigger piece of carrot if you got 1/5 or 1/10?

Activity 3: Measuring

1. When putting the vegetables into the soup, use a variety of measuring cups to demonstrate 1/4 cup, 1/2 cup, 1 cup.

2. Add salt and pepper and other seasonings with measuring spoons.

Activity 4: Counting

1. Have students take turns stirring the soup by counting a certain number of rotations. Example: Everyone gets to stir 10 rotations.

Name _____

Line Them Up!
■ ■ ■ ■ ■ ■ ■ ■ ■ ■ ■ ■

Directions:
1. Look at the order of the fruits and vegetables.
2. Draw what comes next.

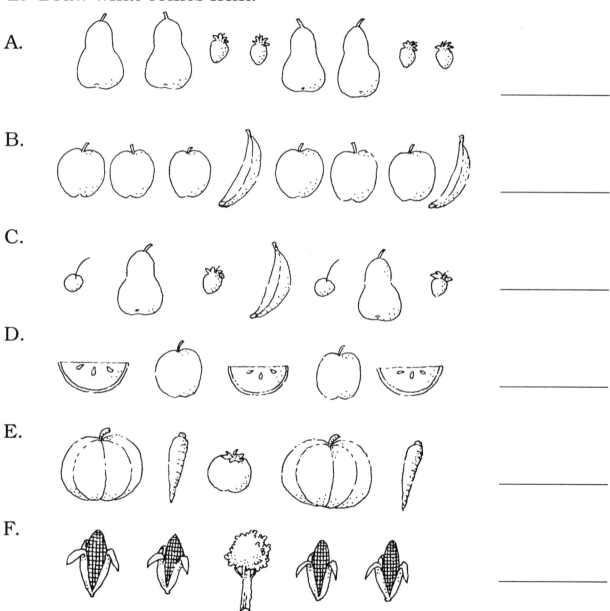

A. _____

B. _____

C. _____

D. _____

E. _____

F. _____

Make your own fruit and vegetable picture problems on the back.
Give them to a friend to solve.

■ ■ ■ ■ **58** ■ ■ ■ ■

Science

■ **Animal Body Coverings** ■
(Animal Classification & Adaptation)

Directions:

1. On a large chart, copy the boxes and questions below.

2. As a class, draw simple pictures of farm animals that have each type of body covering.

3. Discuss how the body covering is useful.

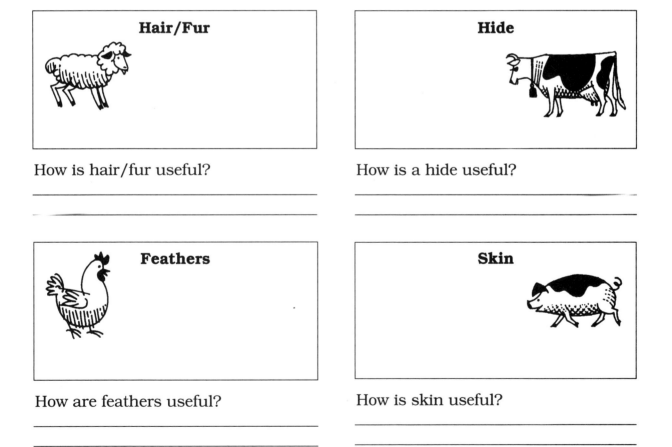

Hair/Fur

How is hair/fur useful?

Hide

How is a hide useful?

Feathers

How are feathers useful?

Skin

How is skin useful?

■ Farm Food Chains ■

Directions:

1. Copy the boxes below on a large chart.

2. Discuss with students how farm animals are both **consumers** and **producers** in the **food chain.**

cow **produces**:
milk, meat, leather

sun and rain help grass grow   cow **consumes** grass

3. Illustrate how these animals are both consumers and producers.

	CONSUME	PRODUCE
Pig		
Chicken		
Sheep		

4. Show how people are both consumers and producers.

	CONSUME	PRODUCE

▦ Farm Animal Characteristics ▦
(Animal Classification)

Directions:

1. Copy the chart below on a large sheet of butcher paper.

2. As a class, discuss the animals and the characteristics listed.

3. If an animal has a certain characteristic, mark an X under that category (for example, a cat has claws).

	hoofs	snout	claws	whiskers	fur	wings	feathers	tail	horns
cat			X	X	X			X	
sheep									
pig									
cow									
horse									
chicken									
dog									
goat									
duck									

Critical Thinking:

1. What are some similar characteristics between a dog and a pig?

2. How are a chicken and a horse different?

3. How is a duck like a chicken?

Extension: Play "What Farm Animal Am I?" in paired groups. Without telling one's partner, choose one of the farm animals. Describe the animal to your partner using the characteristics marked with an X on the chart as clues.

Example: I have claws, whiskers, fur and a tail. What farm animal am I? (answer: a cat)

Name _____

Popcorn and Your Five Senses

Pop up some popcorn and take a close-up look at this yummy snack! Working in small groups, write words that describe how the popcorn looks, smells, feels, tastes, and sounds.

What does your **popcorn** look like?

What does your popcorn **smell** like?

What does your popcorn **feel** like?

What does your popcorn **taste** like?

What does your popcorn **sound** like when you eat it?

Music, Art, & Cooking

▨ Music ▨

1. Copy the songs on a large chart. Invite students to draw pictures illustrating the songs.

2. As a class, chant the farm songs together.

3. Clap the beats of the songs.

4. Play with the songs by changing some of the lyrics.
Example: Add some zoo animals to Old MacDonald's farm!

Farm Songs

The Farmer in the Dell

1. The farmer in the dell, the farmer in the dell,
Heigh-o, the derry o, the farmer in the dell.

2. The farmer takes a wife, the farmer takes a wife,
Heigh-o the derry o, the farmer takes a wife.

3. The wife takes a nurse,...

4. The nurse takes a child,...

5. The child takes a dog,...

6. The dog takes a cat,...

7. The cat takes a rat,...

8. The rat takes the cheese,...

9. The cheese stands alone,...

Old MacDonald

1. Old MacDonald had a farm E-I-E-I-O
And on his farm he had a cow E I-E-I-O
With a moo-moo here and a moo-moo there,
here a moo, there a moo, everywhere a moo-moo,
Old MacDonald had a farm, E-I-E-I-O.

2. And on his farm he had a pig, etc.
With an oink-oink here and an oink-oink there,...

3. And on his farm he had a duck,...
With a quack-quack here and a quack-quack there,...

4. And on his farm he had a donkey,...
With a hee-haw here,...

5. And on his farm he had a horse,...
With a neigh-neigh here,...

6. And on his farm he had some chickens,...
With a cluck-cluck here,...

▦ Art ▦

Scarecrows for Class Crops

Display these scarecrows in "class crops," such as
bean plants or in a class vegetable garden!

Materials:

craft sticks (2 for each scarecrow)
oaktag
3 colors of construction paper
glue
scissors
black markers

Directions:

1. Using oaktag, make templates
of the shirt, head, and hat.

2. Glue two craft sticks together
to form a T.

3. Using the templates, have
students trace the shirt, head
and hat shape using a different
color of construction paper for
each. Cut out.

4. Glue the shapes on the
scarecrow (shirt; head; hat;
add details with a black
marker).

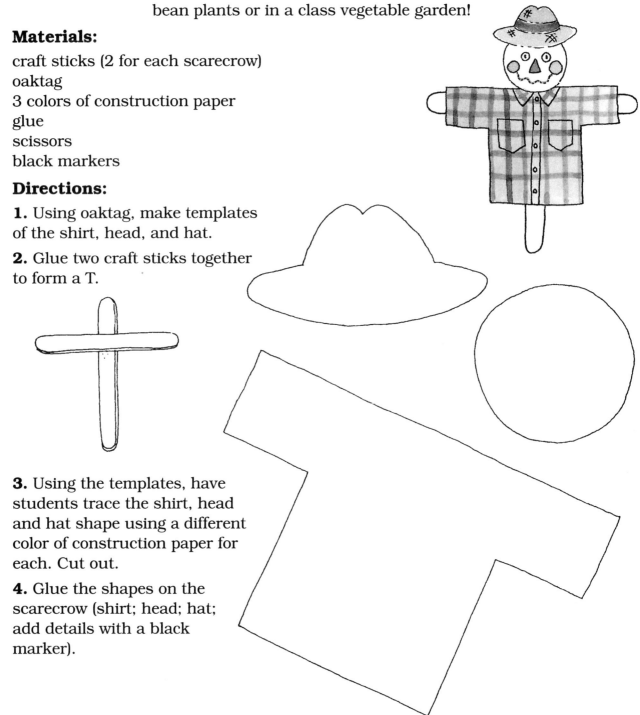

■ Invent a Cereal ■

Students read cereal food labels, then create their own brand of cereal.

Materials:

empty cereal boxes
butcher paper
tape
scissors
scraps of colored
   construction paper
glue
markers and crayons

Directions:

Activity 1: Many nutritious cereals are made from grains. Encourage students to observe a variety of cereal boxes comparing their design, ingredients, and nutrition labels.

Activity 2: Brainstorm the names of cereals with grains in the name. Examples: <u>Corn</u> Flakes, <u>Wheat</u>ies, <u>Rice</u> Krispies. What does it mean if a cereal is *multigrain?*

Activity 3: Cover empty cereal boxes with butcher paper, wrapping them like a gift box. Have students create their own healthy cereal package, using scraps of construction paper, markers, and crayons. Line up the cereal boxes on a shelf ledge or attach them to a bulletin board for a three-dimensional display.

■ Farm Animal Stick Puppets ■

Students will enjoy using these paper-plate puppets
to act out farm stories they have read.

Materials:

scraps of construction paper
   (brown, pink, red,
   white, black, yellow)
tempera paint
   (black, brown, pink)
paint brushes
scissors
cotton balls
glue
stapler
craft sticks

Directions:

1. Before students
make their puppets,
cut eye holes for them
in the paper plates.

2. Students then paint
the paper plates the
color of the animal.
Let dry.

3. Students glue con-
struction paper animal
features to the paper
plates (such as nose,
beak, ears). Glue cot-
ton balls on the sheep's
head.

4. Staple large craft
sticks to the paper
plates.

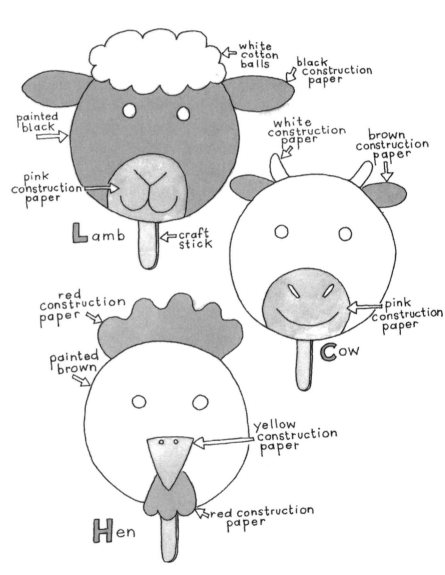

■ Hand-Picked Corn ■

Materials:

glue   yellow and green construction paper
scissors   black markers or crayons

Directions:

1. Have students trace around their tightly held hand on a piece of yellow construction paper. Cut out.

2. Draw kernels (circles) on the corn with a black crayon or marker.

3. Cut out the husk from green construction paper and glue to the corn.

4. Have students put their names on the husk.

5. Display on a bulletin board.

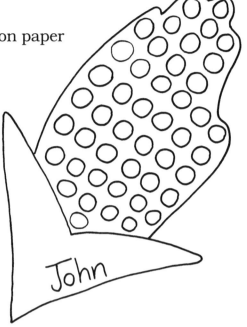

■ Hand-Some Sheep ■

Materials:

black construction paper   cotton balls
"googly" moving eyes   glue
scissors

Directions:

1. Have children trace one of their hands on a piece of black construction paper, keeping the middle three fingers together. The thumb and pinkie should be outstretched slightly.

2. Cut out the sheep shape.

3. Glue cotton balls to the ears.

4. Glue on the moving "googly" eyes.

5. Display the sheep on a bulletin board to frame poems or rhymes about sheep such as "Baa, Baa, Black Sheep" or "Little Bo Peep."

■ Farm Sewing Cards ■

Materials:

lightweight cardboard
scissors
markers
hole punch
shoelaces

Directions:

1. Copy and cut out the farm picture cards (pages 68 and 69).

2. Have students color the farm pictures with markers. Glue to lightweight cardboard. (Laminate the farm pictures for durability.)

3. Punch holes around each picture, as indicated, then knot a shoelace through one hole in each.

4. Students then "sew" a shoelace border around the picture and knot.

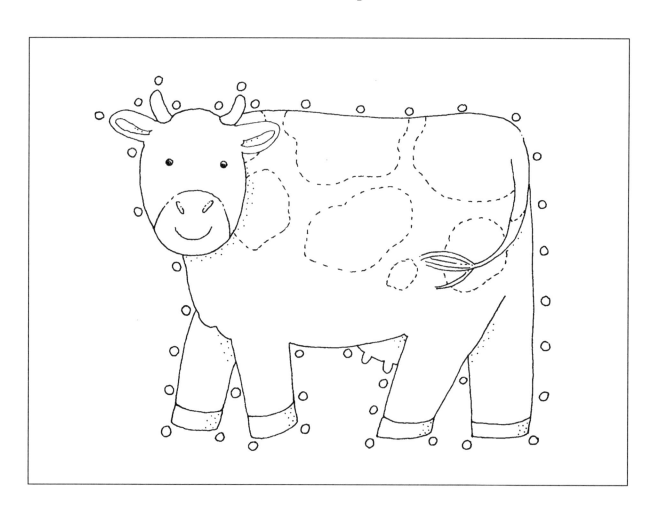

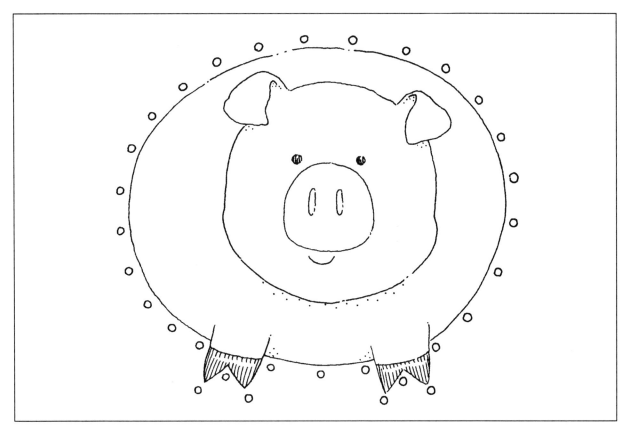

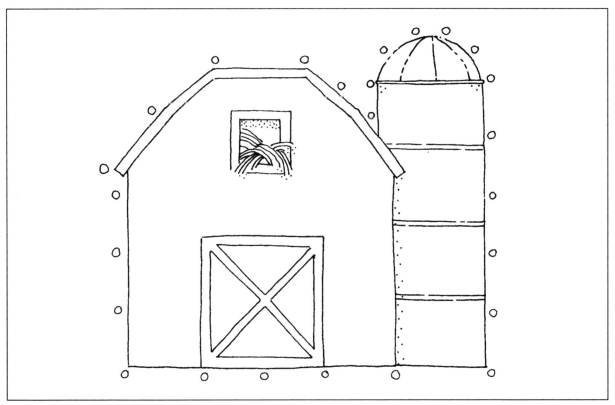

HOMEMADE BUTTER

Ingredients:

2 cups heavy whipping cream
dash of salt (optional)

Directions:

1. Place cream in a mixing bowl.
2. Using an electric mixer, blend cream on high setting until cream turns into butter. Note: An adult should be responsible for use of the electric mixer.

HAYSTACKS

Ingredients:

1 12-oz. package butterscotch pieces
1 12-oz. can of chow mein noodles
1 12-oz. can of peanuts

Directions:

1. Melt butterscotch pieces in a crockpot or microwave.
2. Add chow mein noodles and peanuts. Stir.
3. Drop the haystacks a teaspoon at a time on waxed paper.
4. Cool.

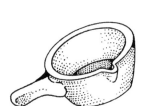

DIRT FOR DESSERT

Ingredients:

paper cups   chocolate-cream sandwich cookies
plastic flowers   optional: gummi-worms
spoons
5 3.4-oz. boxes chocolate pudding mix

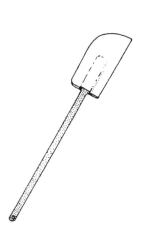

Directions:

1. Follow package directions to make pudding ahead of time.
2. Fill half of each cup with pudding. Mix some "gummi-worms" into the pudding.
3. Crumble cookies over the pudding to look like dirt.
4. "Plant" the flower in the cup.

Puzzles & Games

▓ Barnyard Bingo ▓

Directions:

1. Make copies of the Barnyard Bingo board (page 72). Make one copy for each student or cooperative group.

2. Write the numbers 1 to 25 on each Bingo board, but in varying order.

3. Use the Master Calling Card (page 73) to call numbers (example: cow 3, chicken 6). Put an "X" in each box to keep track of those you've called.

4. Beans can be used as markers to cover the numbers.

5. The game is over when one player has five numbers covered in a row—horizontally, vertically, or diagonally—and says, "Bingo"!

TIP: Laminate the Barnyard Bingo boards and Master Calling Card and place in a math center for small groups.

2	18	9	1	21
25	14	23	6	16
11	17	5	8	20
4	22	15	3	12
19	24	7	10	13

1	24	17	3	12
22	19	8	25	5
2	7	11	21	14
20	13	18	6	10
15	4	9	16	23

■ Barnyard Bingo ■

■ Master Calling Card ■
(Barnyard Bingo)

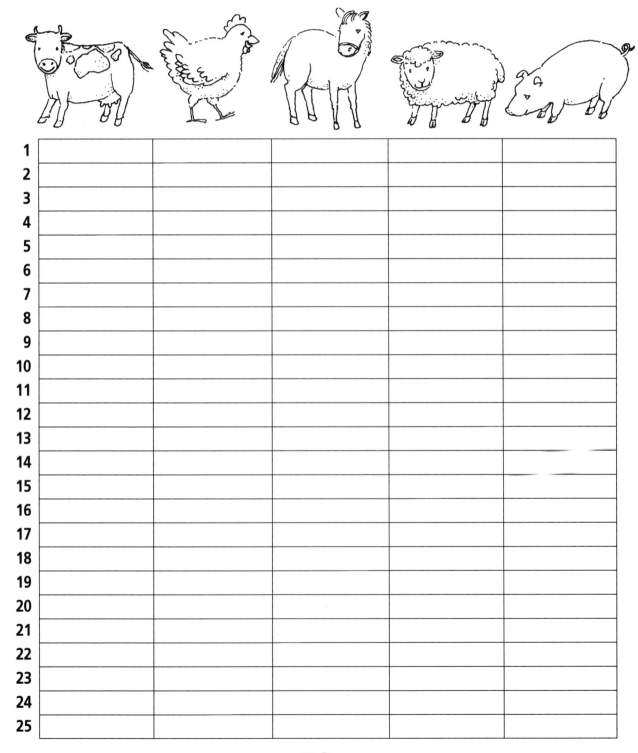

1				
2				
3				
4				
5				
6				
7				
8				
9				
10				
11				
12				
13				
14				
15				
16				
17				
18				
19				
20				
21				
22				
23				
24				
25				

■ Back to the Barn ■
(Addition File Folder Game)

Directions:

1. Copy the game board and the "How to Play" card below.

2. If desired, color the game board for added appeal.

3. Glue the game board and "How to Play" card to a file folder. Optional: Laminate for durability.

4. Assemble two number cubes and markers for players. (Use different kinds of seeds or beans for markers.)

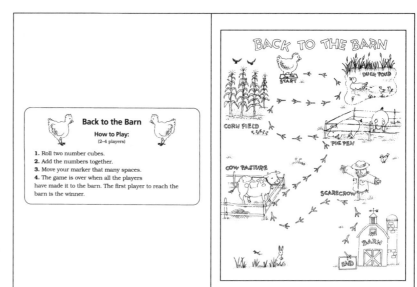

Back to the Barn

How to Play:
(2–4 players)

1. Roll two number cubes.

2. Add the numbers together.

3. Move your marker that many spaces.

4. The game is over when all the players have made it to the barn. The first player to reach the barn is the winner.

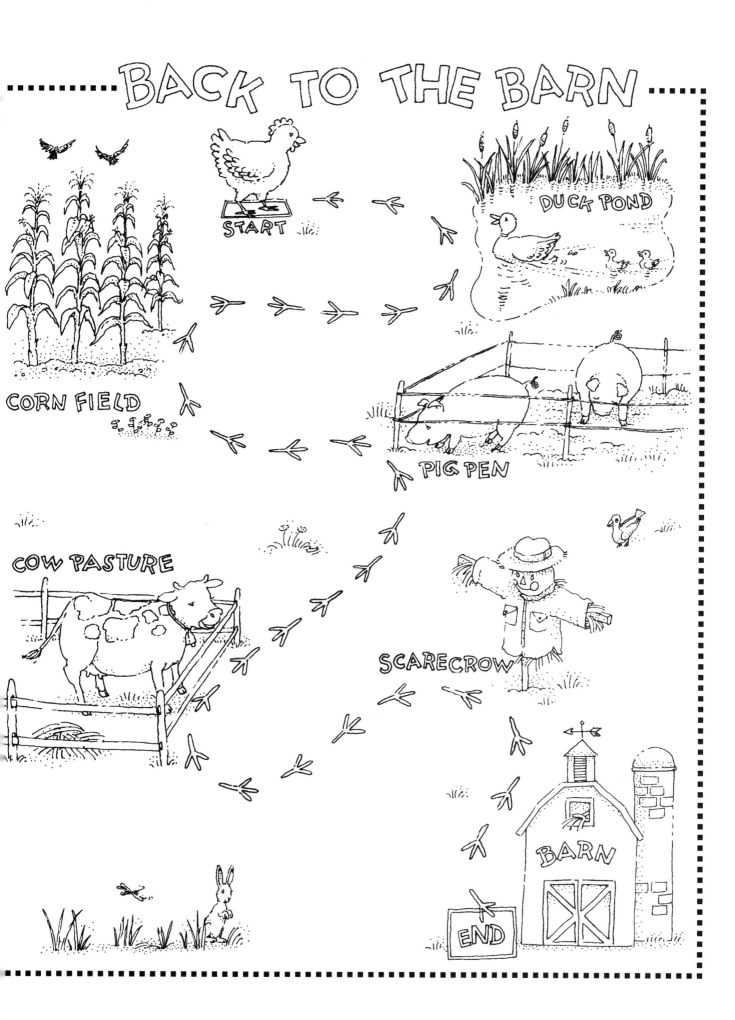

■ Barnyard Animal Concentration ■
(Matching Adult and Baby Animals)

Materials:

3-by 5-inch index cards   scissors

glue   markers

Directions:

1. Copy the "How to Play" card and the Barnyard Animal Concentration Cards (pages 77 and 78).

2. Cut out each animal card and the "How to Play" card.

3. Glue each animal card to half of an index card. If desired, color for added appeal and laminate all of the materials for durability.

4. Store Barnyard Animal Concentration Cards in a ziplock bag.

 # How to Play:
(for 2 players)

1. Lay all the cards face down so that you cannot see the animals.

2. Each player gets a chance to turn over any two cards, trying to match the adult animal with the baby animal. Read the animal names aloud.

3. If the player gets a match, then he or she gets another chance. If not, the next player tries to get a match.

4. The game is over when players have picked up all of the cards.

5. The player with the most barnyard animal matches wins the game!

Pig	Piglet	Goat
Cat	Kitten	Kid
Sheep	Lamb	Hen

Chick	Cow	Calf
Goose	Gosling	Colt
Dog	Puppy	Horse

 # Resources

■ Literature ■

Aylesworth, Jim	**My Son John**, Henry Holt, 1994
Azarian, Mary	**A Farmer's Alphabet**, David R. Godine, 1981
Barrett, Judi	**Cloudy With a Chance of Meatballs**, Macmillan, [1978] 1982
Bellville, Rod and Cheryl W.	**Large Animal Veterinarians**, Carolrhoda, 1983
Brown, Margaret Wise	**Big Red Barn**, HarperCollins, [1956] 1989
	The Little Farmer, Addison-Wesley, 1948
	The Summer Noisy Book, HarperCollins, [1951] 1993
Cauley, Lorinda Bryan	**The Town Mouse & the Country Mouse**, Putnam, (1984) 1990
Cazet, Denys	**Nothing at All**, Orchard Books, 1994
de Paola, Tomie	**Charlie Needs a Cloak**, Simon & Schuster, 1982
	Country Farm, Philomel, 1984
	The Popcorn Book, Holiday House, 1978
Ehlert, Lois	**Eating the Alphabet, Fruits and Vegetables From A to Z**, Harcourt Brace, 1989
	Growing Vegetable Soup, Harcourt Brace, 1990
Ehrlich, Amy	**Parents in the Pigpen, Pigs in the Tub**, Dial, 1992
Freedman, Russell	**Farm Babies**, Holiday House, 1981
Gackenbach, Dick	**Crackle, Gluck and the Sleeping Toad**, Seabury Press, 1979
	The Pig Who Saw Everything, Houghton Mifflin, 1978
Galdone, Paul	**The Little Red Hen**, Clarion, [1973] 1985
Gammell, Stephen	**Once Upon MacDonald's Farm**, Macmillan, 1990
Gibbons, Gail	**Farming**, Holiday House, 1988
	The Milk Makers, Macmillan, [1985] 1987
Haas, Jessie	**Mowing**, Greenwillow, 1994
Hall, Donald	**Ox-Cart Man**, Puffin, 1983
Hutchins, Pat	**Rosie's Walk**, Macmillan, [1968] 1971
Jackson, Ellen B.	**Brown Cow, Yellow Grass, Yellow Mellow Sun**, Hyperion, 1995
Kessler, Ethel and Leonard	**Are There Hippos on the Farm?**, Simon & Schuster, 1986

Lesser, Carolyn	***What a Wonderful Day to Be a Cow***, Knopf, 1995
Lobel, Arnold	***Small Pig***, HarperCollins, [1969] 1988
	A Treeful of Pigs, Scholastic, [1979] 1988
London, Jonathan	***Like Butter on Pancakes***, Viking, 1995
Love, D. Anne	***Bess's Log Cabin Quilt***, Holiday House, 1995
Lumley, Kay	***I Can Be an Animal Doctor***, Children's Press, 1985
Marshall, James	***The Three Little Pigs***, Dial, 1989
Martin Jr., Bill and Archambault, John	***Barn Dance***, Henry Holt, [1986] 1988
McGee, Marni	***The Quiet Farmer***, Atheneum, 1991
Maclachlan, Patricia	***What You Know First***, HarperCollins, 1995
Miller, Jane	***Farm Alphabet Book***, Scholastic, 1987
	Farm Counting Book, Simon & Schuster, 1992
	Seasons on the Farm, Prentice-Hall, 1986
Noble, Trinka Hakes	***The Day Jimmy's Boa Ate the Wash***, Puffin, [1980] 1993
Peters, Lisa Westberg	***Hayloft***, Dial, 1995
Potter, Beatrix	***The Tale of Peter Rabbit***, Puffin, [1902] 1992
Provensen, Alice and Martin	***Our Animal Friends at Maple Hill Farm***, Random House, [1974] 1992
Roop, Peter	***Go Hog Wild! Jokes From Down on the Farm***, Lerner, 1994
Rounds, Glen	***Old MacDonald Had a Farm***, Holiday House, 1989
Stevenson, James	***Could Be Worse!***, William Morrow, 1987
Waddell, Martin	***Farmer Duck***, Candlewick Press, 1992
Wormell, Mary	***Hilda Hen's Happy Birthday***, Harcourt Brace, 1995

■ Poetry ■

Mark Daniel, compiler	***A Child's Treasury of Animal Verse***, Dial, 1989
Meish Goldish	***Animal Poems From A to Z***, Scholastic, 1994
Lee Bennett Hopkins, compiler	***On the Farm***, Little Brown, 1991
Jack Prelutsky, compiler	***The Random House Book of Poetry for Children***, Random House, 1983